I know I Can!
Set the Table

ANTHEA DAVIDSON-JARRETT
Illustrated by
Aldana Penayo
Published by EDUCATE THE GLOBE,
London, UK, 2023.

ISBN: 978-1-913804-07-7

Copyright © 2023 Educate The Globe Limited. All rights reserved. No part of this book is to be reprinted, copied or stored in retrieval systems of any type, except by written permission from the author. Part of this book may, however, be used only in reference to support related documents or subjects.

Artwork featured: Buckley, Omar (2011) Taharqa with Wife and Son at Jebel Barkel; Temple of Mut, Ramomar NY, New York.

I know I can do it!

Please can I help?

I want to do it all by myself!

Please can I try?

Can you show me how?

I'm not too small,

I am ready right now!

Daddy is hosting

a dinner party

for his friends

who are quite arty.

Nhalia is making

lots of food

so everyone can eat

and feel good!

It's nearly time

for daddy's friends to arrive

so daddy wants to set

the table for five.

I want to learn

so that when

I have a party

I can set it up for ten!

First, we change the cloth

for the table.

I can't do this by myself

but Nhalia is able.

Next we lay the place mats

then the dinner plates.

Place them in the middle.

This is looking great!

The plates for the salad

lay on the dinner plates.

The bowls for the soup

sit on the two plates straight.

We fold the napkins neatly.

They'll go on the mat to the left.

I didn't know that!

Nhalia is the best!

Place the forks on the napkins

then the knives go

with the spoons on the right...

just like so!

The glasses of drinking water

Stand above the knives.

The glasses for drinking wine

go above those; to the right.

If you want to,

you can add name tags

at each seat

above the place mats.

Now I know

how to set a table.

It's so easy

and now I am able!

Daddy's friends

will have a great time.

The food is delicious

and the art will be sublime!

www.ingramcontent.com/pod-product-compliance
Lightning Source LLC
Chambersburg PA
CBHW041245240426
43670CB00027B/2996